CRUK.50p
W 44

OWZAT!

looks at Cricket Umpires

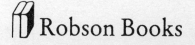
GW00357201

Robson Books

First published in Great Britain in 1987 by Robson Books Ltd,
Bolsover House, 5-6 Clipstone Street, London W1P 7EB.

Copyright © 1987 Larry

British Library Cataloguing in Publication Data

Larry
  Owzat. Larry looks at cricket umpires.
  1. English wit and humor, Pictorial
  Rn: Terence Parkes I. Title
  741.5'942   NC1479

ISBN 0-86051-454-4

All rights reserved. No part of this publication may be
reproduced, stored in a retrieval system, or transmitted in
any form or by any means, electronic, mechanical, photo-
copying, recording or otherwise, without the prior
permission in writing of the publishers.

Made and printed in Great Britain
by the Guernsey Press Co. Ltd., Guernsey, Channel Islands.

FOREWORD

MAN IN THE MIDDLE
by
DICKIE BIRD, MBE
Test and World Cup Final Umpire

People forget that I did play county cricket for Yorkshire and Leicestershire County Cricket Clubs, and lots of people think that I have always been an umpire.

How did I become a County and Test Umpire? When my father died in 1969, I returned to Yorkshire for his funeral. After the funeral I went to watch Yorkshire play at Headingley. A few of the Yorkshire cricketers asked me if I missed playing county cricket. I said I did. They said to me, 'Why don't you go on the First Class Umpires list?' I had never given umpiring a thought. I went home and wrote to Lords to apply for the First Class Umpires list and I was accepted in 1969. That's how it all started.

Umpiring is not easy, it is a job you must try to enjoy. I think it is the next best thing to playing the game. I always try to enjoy my umpiring because by doing that, it helps me to relax.

One or two important things about umpiring. You must have application, dedication, concentration and common sense. You must respect the players and treat them as professional men. If the umpire can gain the respect of the players that is half the battle. You must also learn to live with your mistakes. You are then almost there as an umpire. Everyone makes mistakes in life.

When you are out there in the middle so many funny things happen. I remember umpiring in a Test Match at Old Trafford, England v West Indies. I urgently wanted to use the toilet, so I stopped the Test Match and I said to the players, 'I am very sorry gentlemen but nature calls,' and off I ran to the toilet, to the amusement of the players and a tremendous roar from the crowd.

It is so nice to be asked to do the foreword to *Owzat* by Larry. I cannot pretend to know where his book gets its inspiration from, but am certain that anyone who has ever played a game or two of cricket will relish the humour. I would like to wish the book every success, and to wish all umpires throughout the world every success for the future.

BOW TIE, WHITE GLOVES —
HE'S BEEN STUDYING THE
SNOOKER REFS

I CAN REMEMBER UMPIRING A MATCH
WHEN BENSON AND HEDGES, TWO
TOBACCONISTS, OPENED FOR MIDDLESEX

THAT OVAL MEDAL'S FOR
UMPIRING FOR FIFTY YEARS
AT THE GASWORKS END

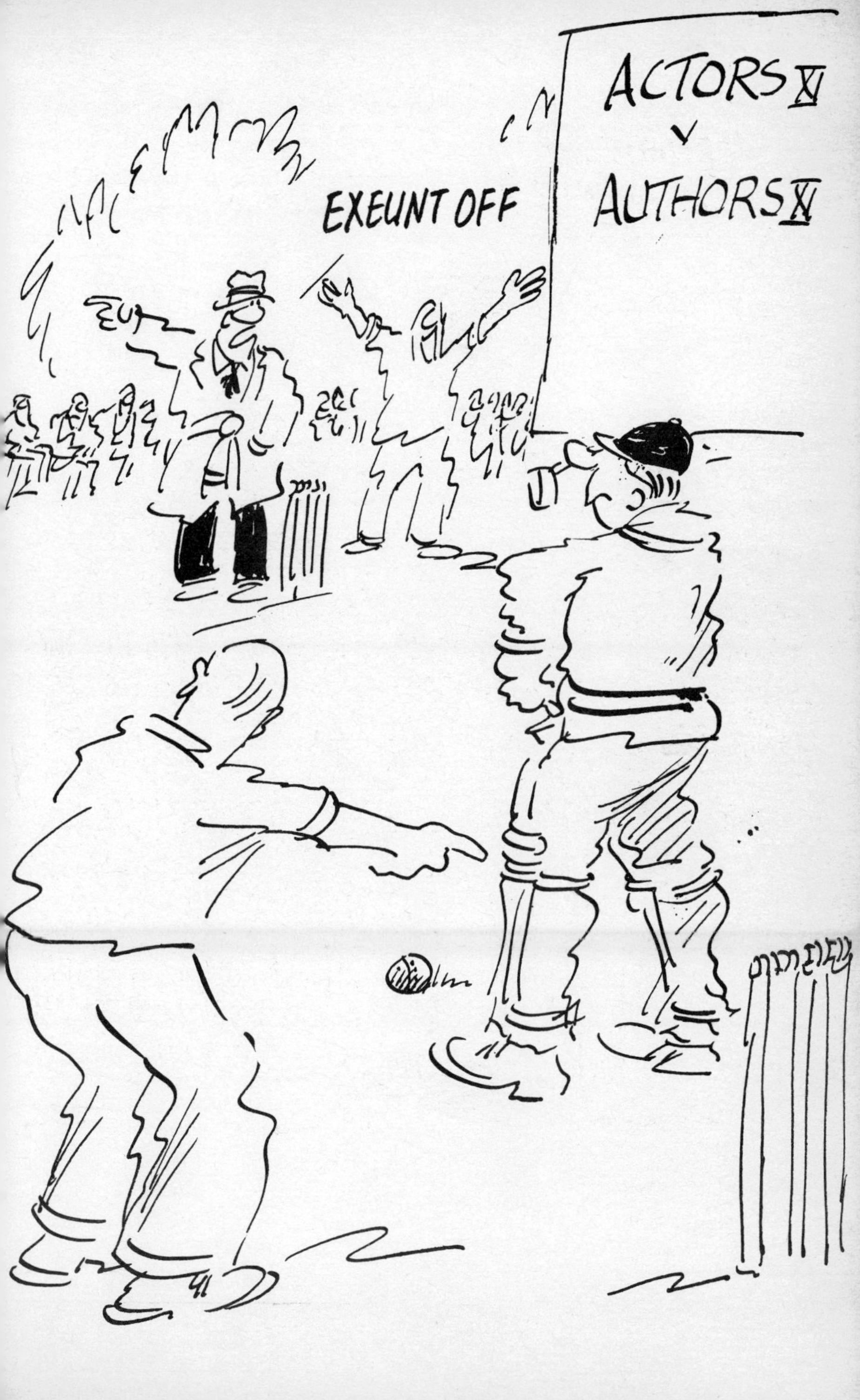
EXEUNT OFF
ACTORS XI
v
AUTHORS XI

HE ALWAYS DID LIKE
TO BE IN THE OUTFIELD

JOHN
HARRIS
COUNTY
CRICKETER
DIED

AS UMPIRES GO, HE
WAS ONE OF THE BEST

I DO LIKE TO SEE
A BALL WELL STRUCK

THEY SAID HE WAS
GOING TO BE DROPPED
FOR THE THIRD TEST
MATCH

HE CALLS HIMSELF A LEPIDOPTERIST
BUT I KNOW WHAT I CALL HIM

GIVE ME MIDDLE, WILL YOU?

IT WAS THE LADIES' TEAM CAPTAIN SHOWING THEIR APPRECIATION OF MY UMPIRING

ONLY HORSES AND UMPIRES CAN SLEEP STANDING UP

CLERGYMEN CRICKETERS

PRISON CRICKET

AND WILL YOU, IF YOU DON'T MIND, UMPIRE AT THE EXECUTION YARD END

WE'RE PROBABLY PLACING THE PITCH OVER AN OLD ESCAPE TUNNEL

SICKNESS

I'VE MADE OUT MY WILL
AND I'M LEAVING YOU MY
BEST WHITE COAT

UMPIRES WEDDINGS

TILL BAD LIGHT
STOPS YOUR PLAY

I LOVE TO SEE FELLOWS
GET MARRIED IN UNIFORM

UMPIRES WEDDING NIGHT

MUSICIANS XI

FINE TIME FOR
THE FLAUTIST
TO BE PRACTICING!

LOOKS LIKE THEY'RE
FIELDING A FULL
ORCHESTRA !

LADIES CRICKET

THEIR FAST BOWLER COULDN'T GET A BABY SITTER

SHE SHOULDN'T PLAY IN HAIR CURLERS

I STILL SAY
IT WASN'T
LBW

IF UMPIRES HAVE A
DISCIPLINARY COMMITEE,
I'LL REPORT HIM TO IT!

OPERA SINGERS XI

LESS OF THIS PRIMA DONNA BEHAVIOUR JUST BECOUSE I'VE REFUSED YOUR LBW APPEAL

ARTISTS MATCH

TOUCH OF ALIZARINE
CRIMSON, I IMAGINE

IT'S WHAT YOU CALL
WORKING ON A
BROAD CANVAS

MP CRICKETERS

AT LAST YOU'VE
CAUGHT THE
SPEAKER'S EYE

WM10
106.26